How to Dream Workbook

Creative Activities to Help You Take the Next Step Towards Freedom

Deedee Cummings

Copyright © 2024 Deedee Cummings

All rights reserved. No part of this publication may be reproduced, distributed, or transmitted in any form or by any means, including photocopying, recording, or other electronic or mechanical methods, without the prior written permission of the publisher, except in the case of brief quotations embodied in critical reviews and certain other noncommercial uses permitted by copyright law. For permission requests, write to the publisher, addressed "Attention: Permissions Coordinator," at the address below.

Published in the United States by Make A Way Media, LLC

ISBN: 978-1-951218-54-6 (Paperback)
ISBN: 978-1-951218-46-1 (epub)

Names and details of the author's clients mentioned in this text have been changed to protect their confidentiality. The names of some things and places are made up by the author to use for demonstration only.
Every effort has been made to properly attribute quotes and summarize background stories correctly.

Workbook design by Molly Ippolito
mollyippolito.com

Printed in the United States of America.
First printing edition 2024
Make A Way Media, LLC
104 Daventry Lane
Louisville, KY 40223

www.makeawaymedia.com

About the Author

Deedee Cummings is a professional dreamer. She is also an author of nineteen books, therapist, attorney, and mom from Louisville, Kentucky. Cummings founded Make A Way Media in 2014 after struggling to find books with characters who looked like her own children and an extreme lack of stories that reflected their life experiences. Books published by Make A Way focus on hope, diversity, social justice, and therapeutic skills for children and adults.

Her work has been featured in HuffPost, Forbes, NPR, USA Today, Essence Magazine, Psych Central, Well+Good, and The EveryGirl, among other media outlets. In 2021, she was appointed to the Kentucky Early Childhood Advisory Council by Kentucky Governor Andy Beshear acknowledging her decades long service to the children and families of Kentucky. Cummings is also the founder of The Louisville Book Festival. She was inspired to work to highlight and celebrate a culture of reading in her community after working as an in-home therapist and visiting homes of children who had no books. Cummings believes literacy is a fundamental human right. Her work highlights inspiring messages that remind us all it is never too late to begin again. She is currently working to adapt her latest children's series inspired by the life of her daughter, Kayla Pecchioni (a Broadway actress) to a Broadway musical. Cummings recently founded the **Make A Way Mindset** program to teach the unshakable mindset she has developed as an entrepreneur of thirty years. She lives with her husband Anthony and has three children Kayla, Anthony, and Nick.

Other Books by the Author

Books for kids

Love Is…
Think of it Like This!
My Trip to the Beach
My Dad's Job
Heart
I Want to be a Bennett Belle
If a Caterpillar Can Fly, Why Can't I?
Like Rainwater
This is The Earth
In The Nick of Time
Kayla: A Modern-Day Princess
Kayla: A Modern-Day Princess—Dishes, Dancing, and Dreams
Kayla: A Modern-Day Princess—Tough as Tulle
Kayla: A Modern-Day Princess—These Shoes Were Made for Dancing
Kayla: A Modern-Day Princess—A Little Magic
Kayla: A Modern-Day Princess Activity Book
In the Nick of Time Too

Books for adults and young adults

How to Dream
How to Dream Workbook

Introduction

How do you dream in a world that actively crushes dreams?

This workbook accompanies the book **How to Dream** written by Deedee Cummings.

The exercises in this journal are designed to help you rise above life's challenges and live a fuller, happier life.

Success looks different for everyone. My hope is that you find *freedom*. Freedom to live the life of your dreams. That is *true* success.

Make a date with this book and make a commitment to give yourself the space and the time to dream.

You deserve this.

Deedee Cummings

Tips for using the workbook...

- Dedicate a specific time each week to work on the activities.
- Be honest and open with yourself as you explore your wants and your thoughts.
- Revisit and revise your goals and plans as needed.
- Carry this workbook/ journal with you so you always have it when inspiration hits.
- Get a group involved or a partner and go through the book together to stay accountable.
- Use the workbook along with the book *How to Dream* by Deedee Cummings.
- Allow yourself the freedom to **dream**.

Document your dream!

Write your **biggest** dream below.

_____
_____
_____
_____
_____
_____
_____
_____
_____
_____
_____

Sign your name & date

Document your dream!

I know I can achieve this dream because...

_____

_____

_____

_____

_____

_____

_____

_____

_____

_____

_____

You can achieve this dream because:

- You are breathing.
- You are strong.
- You have hope.
- Dreams come true every day. Why not yours?
- You won't stop.

"Your life belongs to you. Dreaming is freedom of the mind, heart, and soul."

—Deedee Cummings

Defining a dream

A dream is:

- freedom.
- life.
- a gift.
- your idea.
- your hope.
- your song.
- your calling.
- your legacy.
- your testimony.
- the reason you are here.
- like air to breathe.
- your passion.
- your purpose.
- fuel.
- everything.
- your ticket to the life you *deserve*, not the life you accept.

Defining a dream

What's your definition of a dream?

_____
_____
_____
_____
_____

What's so special about our dreams?

_____
_____
_____
_____
_____

Defining a dream

Complete the table below. Write down the names of people you admire, their dream, and what you believe their dream has done for them. What kind of life did it allow them to have? When we see the power of dreams in the lives of others, we believe they are possible.

Name	Dream	Results

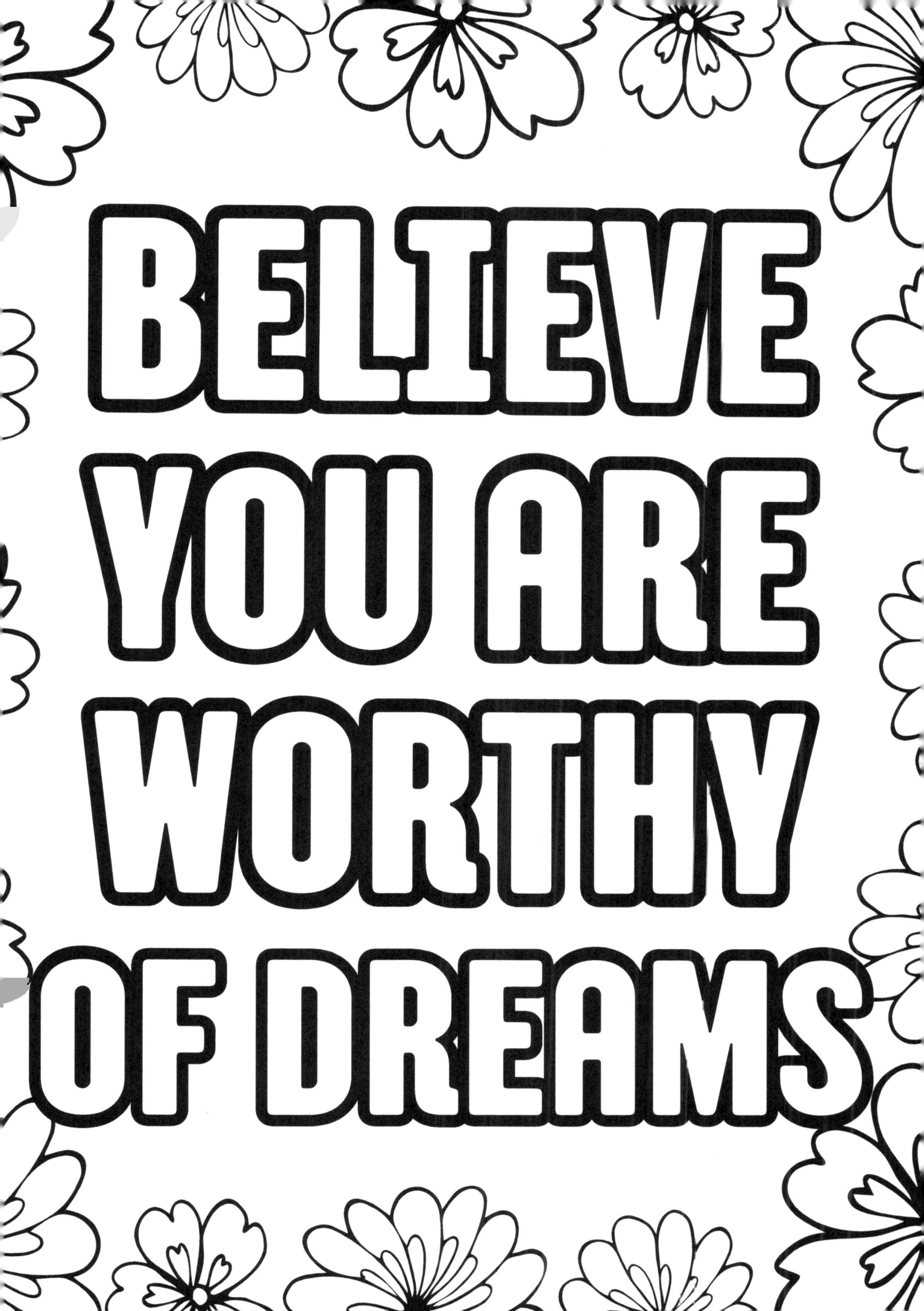

Worthiness

Remember, **YOU** are worthy of your dreams!

Read the sentences below and complete them with your initial thoughts. This list of answers can provide some idea about what makes you happy and what you struggle with. This is powerful insight into what makes you tick!

Repeat this exercise for the next 4 weeks and watch how your responses become more positive over time!

Week 1

- I often look forward to...

- I get my strength from...

- It made me feel great when...

- I find it hard to...

- It makes me angry when...

- I sometimes fear that...

- This week is going to be...

- I flourish when...

- This week I hope to...

Worthiness

Remember, YOU are worthy of your dreams!

Week 2

- I often look forward to…

- I get my strength from…

- It made me feel great when…

- I find it hard to…

- It makes me angry when…

- I sometimes fear that…

- This week is going to be…

- I flourish when…

- This week I hope to…

- What am I learning about myself?

Worthiness

Remember, YOU are worthy of your dreams!

Week 3

- I often look forward to...

- I get my strength from...

- It made me feel great when...

- I find it hard to...

- It makes me angry when...

- I sometimes fear that...

- This week is going to be...

- I flourish when...

- This week I hope to...

- What am I learning about myself?

Worthiness

Remember, YOU are worthy of your dreams!

Week 4

- I often look forward to...

- I get my strength from...

- It made me feel great when...

- I find it hard to...

- It makes me angry when...

- I sometimes fear that...

- This week is going to be...

- I flourish when...

- This week I hope to...

- What am I learning about myself?

Dream board

Have you ever heard of a Vision Board?
Make one right here in this book!
Use these two pages to add your favorite quotes, and pictures of a place you'd like to vacation, the home you want to buy, you in retirement, or college tuition for your kids paid for. You can add whatever you want here and look back on it when you need to be reminded of what you are working for.
Feel free to cover up these words and make
these pages all yours!

Dream board

Visualize your dream and you in it...
what does it look like?
What will it feel like?
Use words and pictures to cover these
pages to keep you inspired.

Bri's Story

Read Bri's story in the book and think about the following questions.

- How hard it can be to break patterns?
- Why is it important to put yourself at the center of your dreams?
- What do you think made Bri gave up on her dream?
- What patterns do YOU notice in your life?
- What can you do to make sure you won't give up on your own dreams?
- What steps can you take to put yourself at the center of YOUR dreams?

Write your thoughts on the lines to refer back to later.

_____
_____
_____
_____
_____

Bri's Story

My dream has purpose!

Identify the top 5 qualities you love most about yourself.

♡ I am... _____

♡ I am... _____

♡ I am... _____

♡ I am... _____

♡ I am... _____

Now, consider your dream. How will these qualities help you make your dream a reality?

_____

_____

_____

_____

If I'm Struggling...

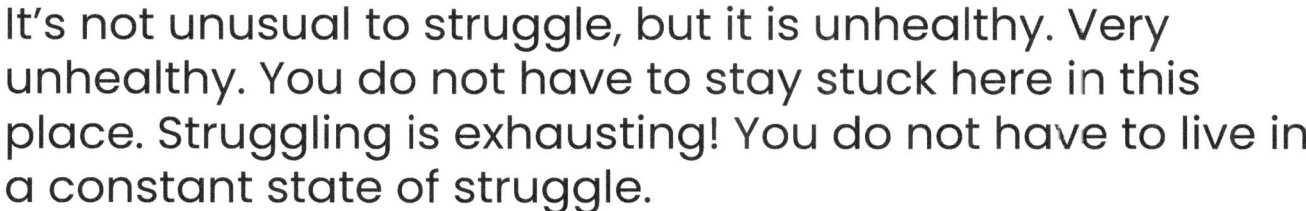

I can make these promises to myself...

- Seek input from a licensed therapist
- Seek advice from a friend who is positive
- Join a positive mindset group
- Journal for clarity & accountability
- Do something completely different

It's not unusual to struggle, but it is unhealthy. Very unhealthy. You do not have to stay stuck here in this place. Struggling is exhausting! You do not have to live in a constant state of struggle.

What promises will you make to yourself to get help believing you are worthy and that you have valuable skills and qualities that already live inside you?

_____
_____
_____
_____
_____
_____
_____
_____
_____

"Roadblocks are not dead ends."
–Deedee Cummings

Obstacles to dreams

Obstacles can interfere with dreams. Practice seeing obstacles as opportunities to learn how to make your dream stronger, not as signs to drop out!
How do you get around roadblocks? Identify one obstacle standing in the way of your dream right now and brainstorm three possible solutions to move past it.

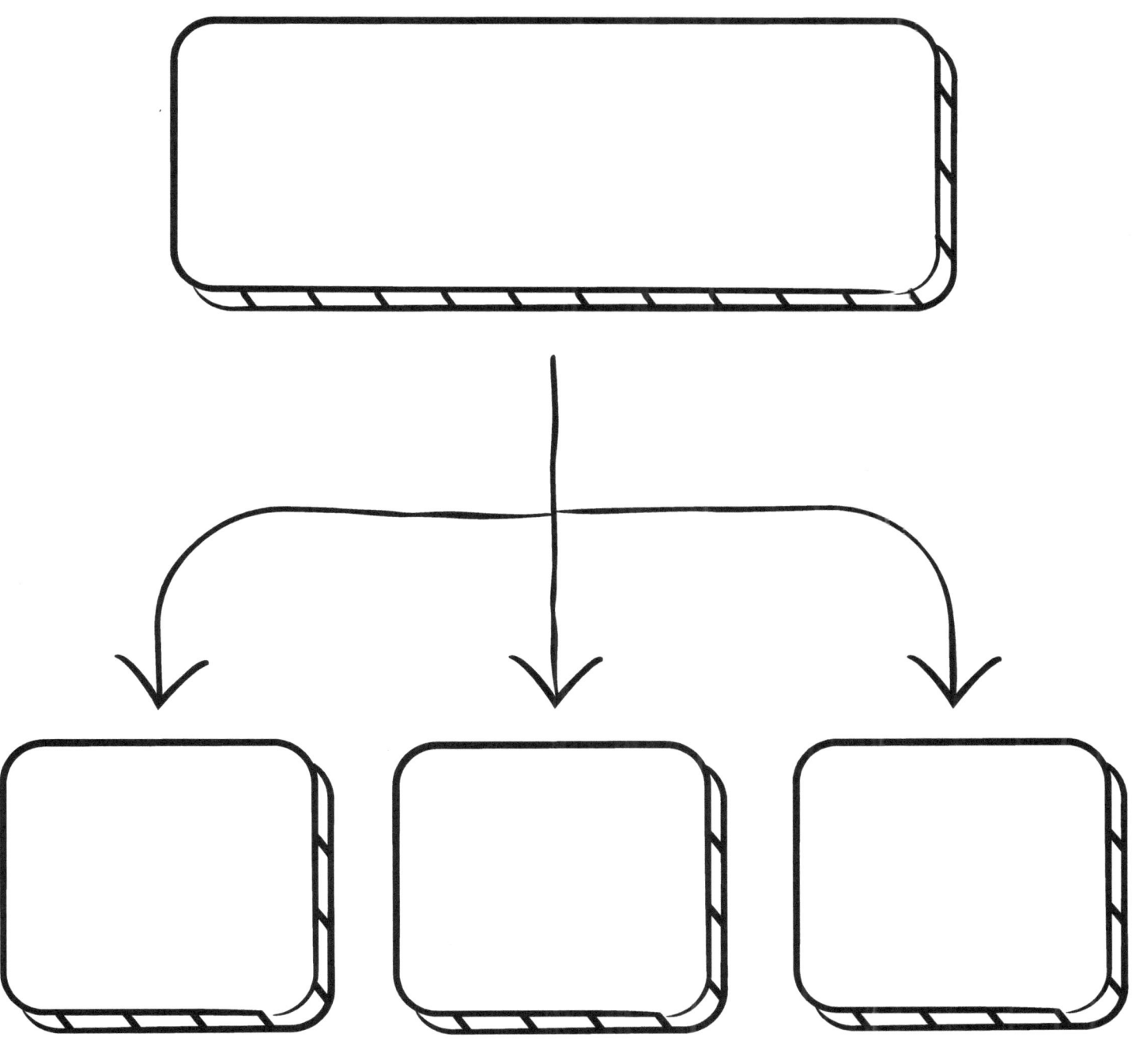

Finding my Passion

What do you *want* your life to look like?

_____
_____
_____
_____
_____
_____

What changes are you willing to make? **Change has to be a part of your plan.** Change changes things.

_____
_____
_____
_____
_____
_____

Tracy's Story

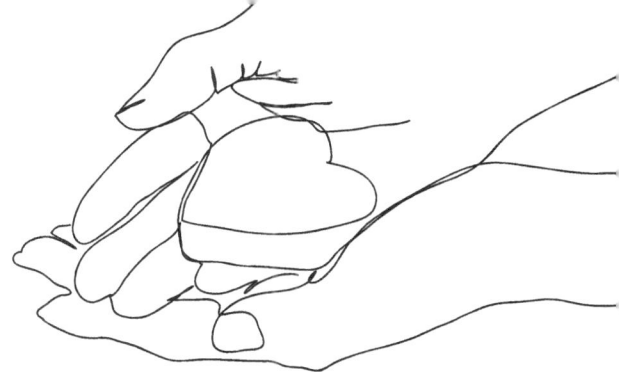

Read Tracy's story in the book and think about the following questions.

- What short-term sacrifices did Tracy make for long-term gains?
- What sacrifices can you can make similar to Tracy?
- Why do you think Tracy felt ungrateful?
- Is it ungrateful to want to become the best version of yourself?
- What other messages do we get about the dangers of dreaming or how selfish it is to want to follow your dream?
- What do you think Tracy's life would have been like if she never believed she could do and be more?

Write your thoughts on the lines to refer back to later.

_____
_____
_____
_____
_____

Tracy's Story

The Best Version of Me

Think about past versions of you. Which version is the best? Write about the "old me" and the "new me" from your own perspective. How they have helped each other or inspired you to keep your dream in motion.

Pouring into You

You cannot pour from an empty cup. Consider ways you can care for yourself and write them below.

Taking time to do these things for **you** is not optional! *This is essential.*

Schedule these things into your day like you would a doctor appointment.

Expect Fear

What are you most afraid of?

_____
_____
_____
_____
_____
_____

We often think in terms of "what is the worst that can happen" but what is the **BEST** that can happen?

_____
_____
_____
_____
_____
_____

"The message fear brings is never as bad as the feeling fear brings."
—Deedee Cummings

Overcoming Fears

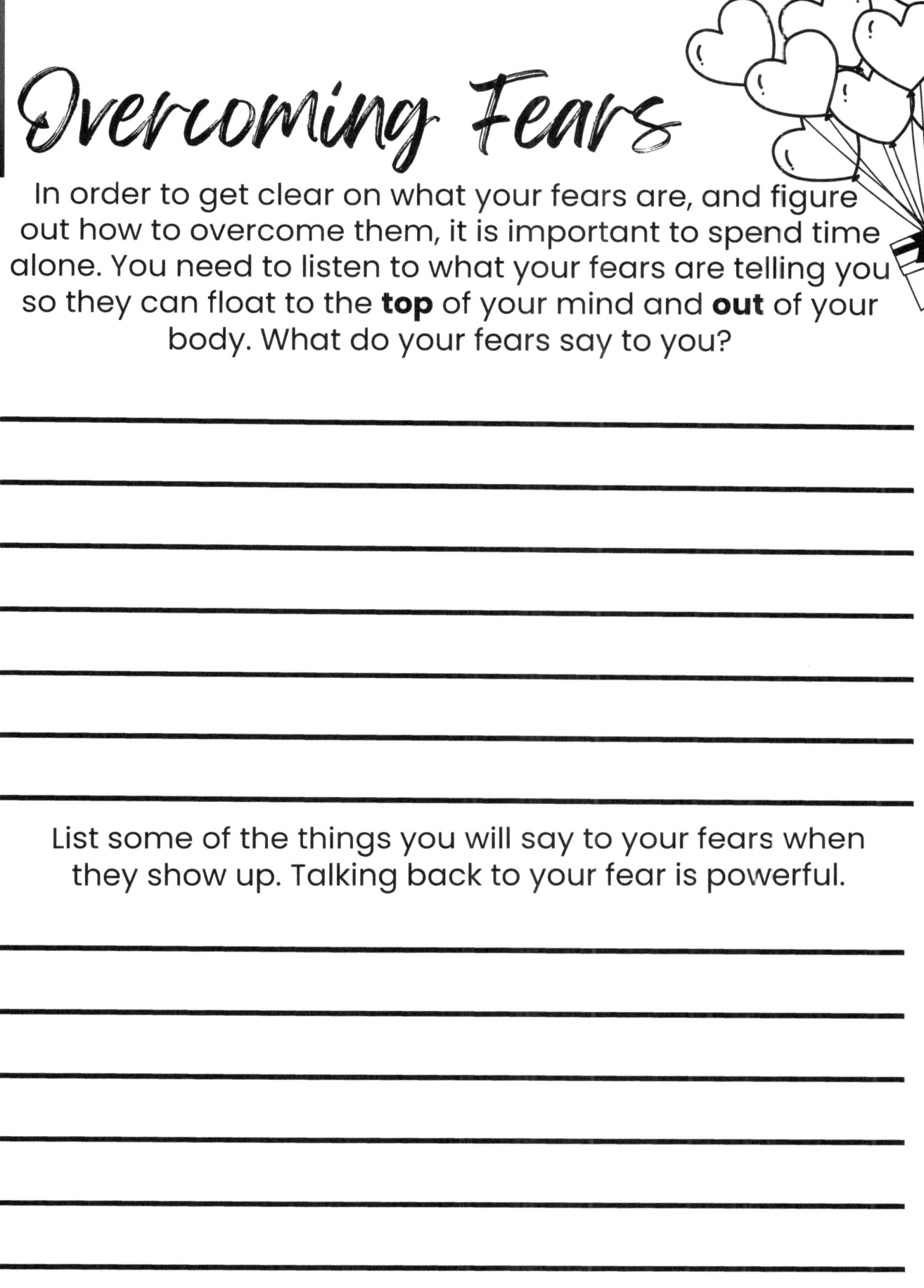

In order to get clear on what your fears are, and figure out how to overcome them, it is important to spend time alone. You need to listen to what your fears are telling you so they can float to the **top** of your mind and **out** of your body. What do your fears say to you?

_____
_____
_____
_____
_____
_____

List some of the things you will say to your fears when they show up. Talking back to your fear is powerful.

_____
_____
_____
_____
_____
_____

Overcoming Fears

The world is loud and getting louder. How will you ever hear your thoughts? How will you ever get to you? Write three blocks of time here that you will start giving to yourself. (Examples are: your 30-minute break, your time in the carpool line, the very first 15 minutes of the day.)

Ways to get to me!

Give yourself these blocks of time!

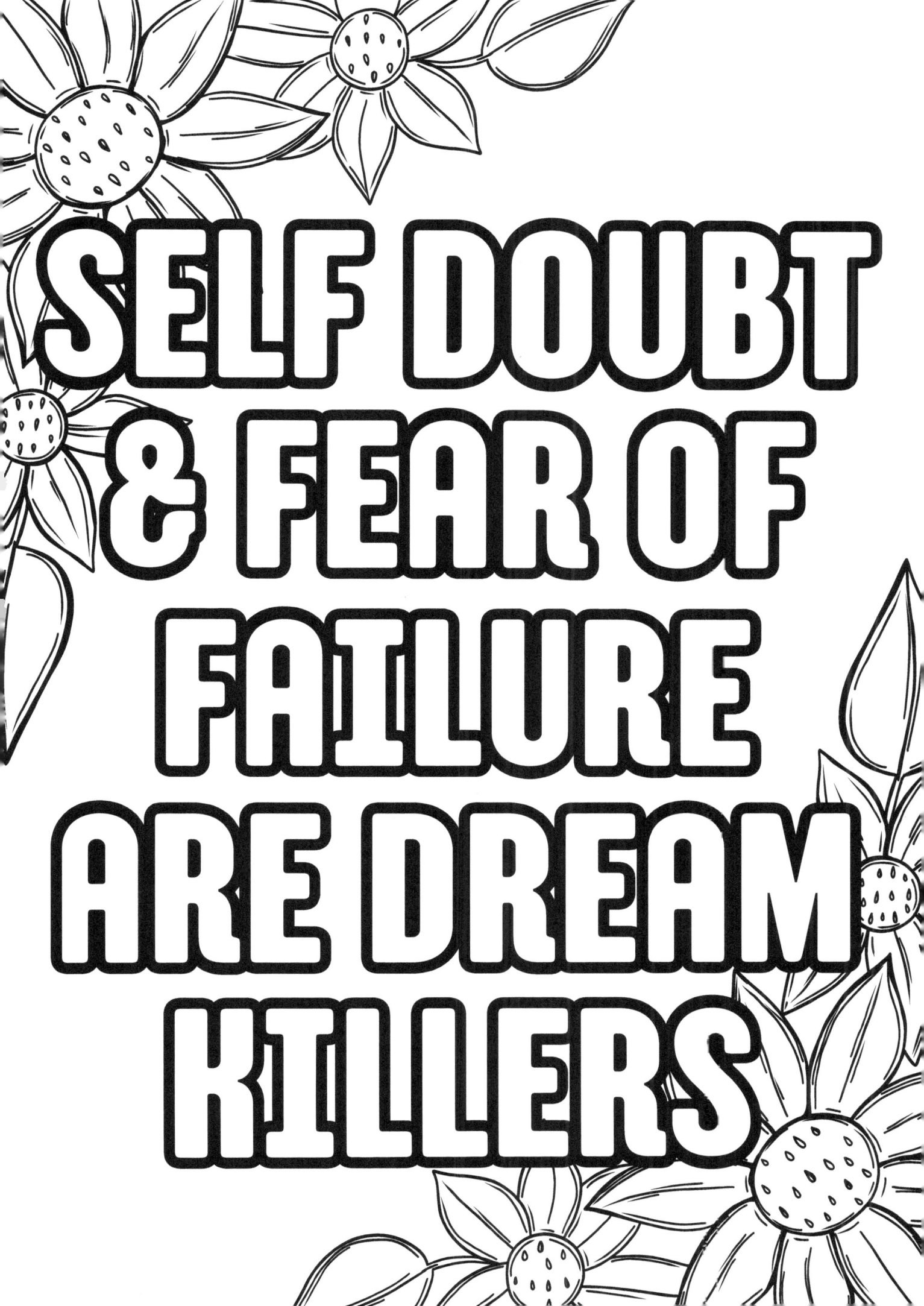

I am the Expert on Me

How do I become confident about who I am and what I want?

YOU are the expert on YOU. No one knows what you need or want better than you do. If you feel confused about where you are on your journey, here are some tips to get you in touch with your aspirations:

 **Spend some time in solitude. Remove all distractions for an extended period of time.**

 **Try writing down your thoughts to clear out the ones that are not helpful and better organize the thoughts that are helpful.**

 **Remind yourself daily with positive affirmations that you have the right to dream and your vision is valid.**

 **Get a little cocky about yourself, your vision, your hopes, and your dream.**

 **Get used to trusting and listening to your internal guide (your gut) to help you decide the next step to take.**

 **Never stop learning or being open to learning and receiving constructive feedback.**

Evidence of Dreams

Evidence that dreams come true every single day is *everywhere*. Just look around you. Feeling discouraged? Count the number of dreams you see on the way home from work or the store. Every sign and invention you see is evidence of a dream.
How many dreams can you see in this image?

Feelings are not Fact

Feelings are not fact but we often act as if they are. It's time to learn to separate the two. Emotions are at the very core of our motivation. **If we cannot tell what is feeling and what is fact we will be knocked off our course much more easily.**

Here is an example: Your partner tells you they don't like the dinner you made. You feel rejected, but the fact is, dinner was burnt! Take the emotion out of it and you will have a completely different outcome. Your partner told you a fact, but you absorbed the fact as a feeling. Laugh about it and go get tacos.

In the book there is an opposite scenario discussed where a feeling is absorbed as fact. Think about times in your life when you have experienced this mix up and how bad it made you feel. It is to your benefit to avoid having this happen again.

Here are some ideas you can explore when you're mixing up facts with feelings.

- Dig into why you feel the way you do. Don't just accept it.
- Ask yourself, "How was this feeling created? Where did it come from?"
- Pull out the fact in the story and focus on that.
- Consider that your feelings may not be accurate.
- What is the story you are telling yourself about the event?
- Ask someone you trust outside of the situation for their perspective.
- Can you rewrite the story and benefit from interpreting what happened in a different way?

"The world is loud. Your dreams have to be louder."

-Deedee Cummings

Set Boundaries with a Dream Killer

Boundaries help separate you from others for protection. Healthy boundaries, especially with people who don't support your dream, are crucial. Let's think about boundaries on a scale of 1 - 10.

0/10
No Boundaries

10/10
Severe Boundaries

Consider the people and connections in your life. Rate the different relationships below on the degree of boundaries **you should** have with them.

People	Degree of Boundary
Family	
Close Friends	
Partner	
Work Colleagues	
Neighbors	
Social Media	

Setting Boundaries 101

Pay attention to how your body feels.
Your body will often feel uneasy before your mind has all the answers figured out.
Take your time and decide what YOU want to do.
The worse people act when you ask for time to think about it, or say no, the more convinced you should be that saying no was
the **right** thing to do.
You are in control of your time and your energy.

All About Distractions

Stay calm. Stay focused. Negativity is a major distraction. Blowing up and becoming angry "because you have the right to" is a distraction, and most often, not worth the energy it takes from your life.

Spend time learning how to **respond**, not react.
- Don't take negativity personally. It is rarely about you. I promise.
- Don't internalize negativity.
- Don't allow it to follow you into your space.
- Shake it off.
- Set it down. Leave it right there, wherever you are.

Try 3-minute breathing!

Minute 1	Answer the question, "How am I doing right now?" Focus on putting your thoughts and feelings into words.
Minute 2	Spend this next minute focusing on your breathing. How fast are you breathing? How slow are you breathing? Be grateful for your breathing.
Minute 3	Use the last minute to control your breathing, exhaling away the negativity as you stretch and expel the negativity from your body and your mind.

Your Phone is a Trap!

If you tell yourself you have no time for your dream, but spend an hour mindlessly scrolling on your phone, **you DO have time for your dream!** It's important to be aware of how much time you spend scrolling. Use the table below to track your screen time for the next 7 days. What do you notice? How can you unplug?

Day	Time Spent Scrolling

You can't become the expert in your field by watching others make moves on social media. It doesn't work that way.

Dreaming can be hard!

Think about the hardest thing you've ever done. Write the choices you had to make to reach your dream. What did you tell yourself to make it through? How did you make it over the hump?

_____
_____
_____
_____
_____
_____
_____

Stay encouraged. You have already done tough things.

Keisha's Story

Read Keisha's story in the book and think about the following questions.

- What do the manager at Keisha's old job and the queen bee of a hive have in common?
- Why do you think Keisha's mom appeared to hold her back? Was she a bad parent?
- What are the statements in your mind that are holding you back?
- What things in your life are holding you back and "keeping you in line"?
- What are three things you can do this month to break up the routine that is your life?

Write your thoughts down on the lines to refer back to later.

_____
_____
_____
_____
_____

Keisha's Story

_____
_____
_____
_____
_____
_____
_____
_____
_____
_____
_____

Let's Journal!

Reflect on the success stories in the book *How to Dream*. What inspiration can you pull from these messages? It is so important that we learn to be inspired by one another, not discouraged. Practice expressing **inspiration** and **hope** now.

_____
_____
_____
_____
_____
_____
_____
_____
_____
_____
_____
_____
_____
_____
_____

Let's Journal!

Lies about Failure

The fear of failing is fueled by the motivation to be perfect and the fear of judgment and ridicule from others. Failure causes us to feel shame, avoidance, and procrastination. **But, the feelings that come with failure are often not fact.** Think of someone who fails and then calls themselves stupid, when they are not stupid at all!

You can be inspired to start a new dream, *even after failure*. Failure transports you to a hill with a view you would have never had if it were not for that failure. **Failure is not an end. Failure is a portal.**

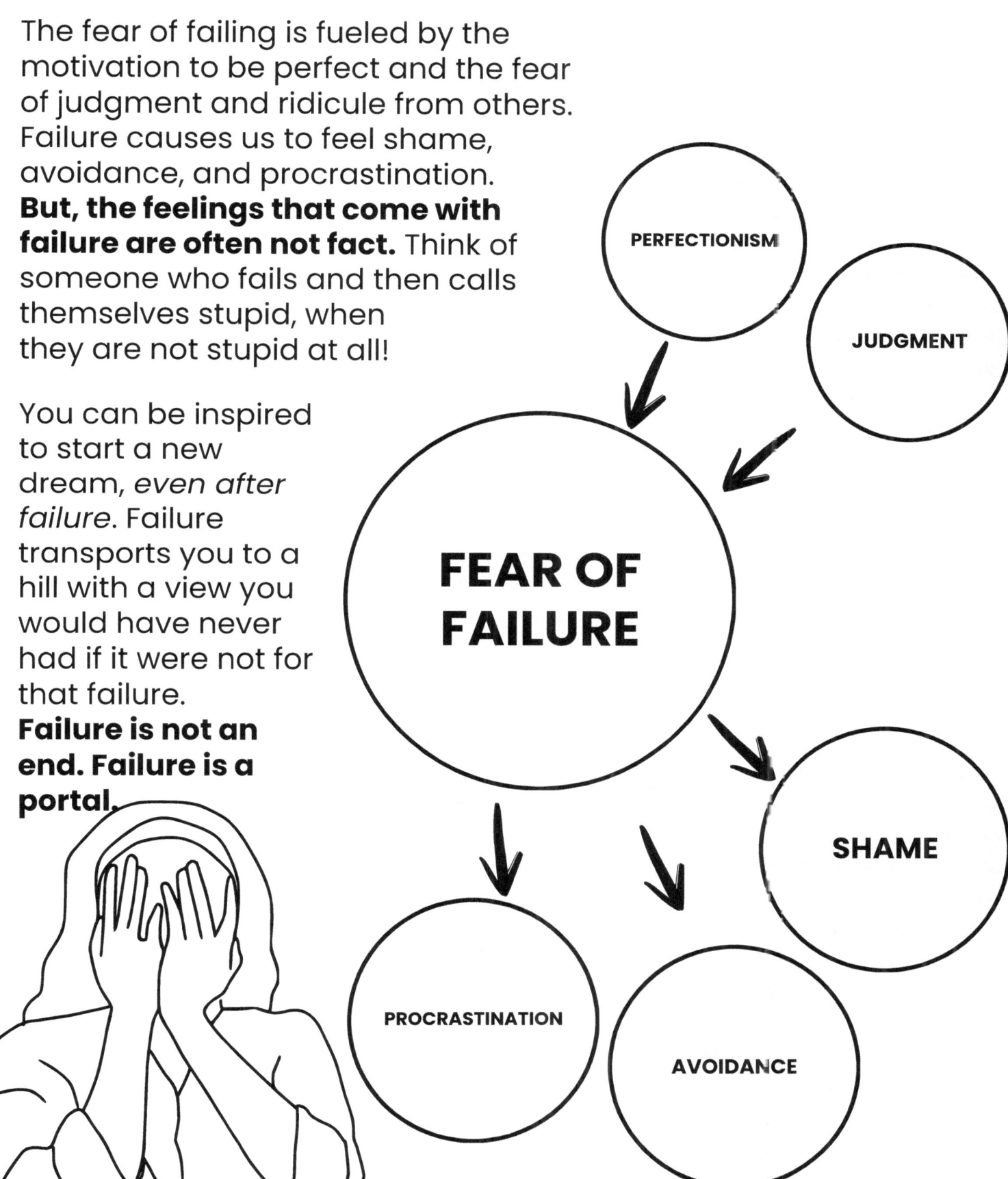

Lies about Failure

Failure transports you to a hill (or maybe a valley) with a view you would have never had if it were not for that failure.

You can overcome the fear of failure by trying a new skill (like dancing, cooking, writing, etc.). When you mess up, try to laugh about it and remind yourself that you will be a student for the rest of your life. It's good to always be learning new things. Make a goal to try something new this month.
Then, reflect on how it went!

This month I will...

The Thing about Dreams

If the dream was not possible, the dream never would have been delivered to you. Use the mind map below to brainstorm why your dream chose you.

Why NOT you? Remember your dream is your gift.

Making it Happen

If your dreams don't scare you, they're not big enough! Rewrite your **BIG** dream below.

_____

_____

_____

_____

☑ Does your dream scare you?

☐ **Yes**   ☐ **No**

Now you have to go get it! Face the fear and do it *anyway*. Make it happen by taking **ONE** step towards your dream each day. Use the strategies below to help if you get stuck!

- Ask for help! If you get a no, ask someone else.
- Join a positive group of like-minded people.
- Be open to change.
- Break your long-term goals into short-term goals.
- Change your approach.
- Never stop working on your *mindset*.
- Practice your affirmations.
- Re-read *How to Dream* and work in this book often.

Go Get it!

Today

What is a list of things you can easily do today to get started on your dream? Complete the check list.
Don't feel pressured to fill up the list for one day!

- [ ] _____
- [ ] _____
- [ ] _____
- [ ] _____
- [ ] _____
- [ ] _____
- [ ] _____
- [ ] _____
- [ ] _____

Go Get it!

Date

What is a list of things you can easily do this week to get started on your dream? Complete the check list.

This week

- [ ] _____
- [ ] _____
- [ ] _____
- [ ] _____
- [ ] _____
- [ ] _____
- [ ] _____
- [ ] _____
- [ ] _____

Go Get it!

Date _____

What is a list of things you can easily do this month to get started on your dream? Complete the check list.

This month

- [ ] _____
- [ ] _____
- [ ] _____
- [ ] _____
- [ ] _____
- [ ] _____
- [ ] _____
- [ ] _____
- [ ] _____

Go Get it!

Date

What is a list of things you can easily do this year to get started on your dream? Complete the check list.

This year

- [ ] _____
- [ ] _____
- [ ] _____
- [ ] _____
- [ ] _____
- [ ] _____
- [ ] _____
- [ ] _____
- [ ] _____

Turn your Dreams into Goals

What are the <u>personal</u> steps you need to take to turn your **dreams** into **goals**?

_____
_____
_____
_____
_____
_____
_____

"Sometimes the journey is more the goal than the goal itself. Take the journey."

Deedee Cummings

Make a Timeline

You need a timeline, so that time does not get away from you, as time often does. Let's plot your dream below. **Add a month or year with a goal in each box.** *This is accountability.*

Don't get Discouraged!

What are things you will *grab, hold on to*, and **remember** along the way that will help you become a better version of yourself than you are today?

_____

_____

_____

_____

_____

_____

_____

_____

_____

_____

_____

_____

_____

A Growth Mindset

A growth mindset is based on the idea that, with hard work and practice, a person's abilities and talents can change and improve over time. On the other hand, a fixed mindset believes that new things can't be learned and things and people will stay pretty much the same.

Write about a time in your life where you acted with a growth mindset.

_____
_____
_____
_____
_____

Write about a time in your life where you acted with a fixed mindset.

_____
_____
_____
_____
_____

A Growth Mindset

Personal affirmations can help us better embrace a growth mindset. Use the table below to brainstorm some affirmations you can tell yourself when things get hard.

I can do this!
_____

_____

_____

_____

_____

_____

_____

_____

A Growth Mindset

Use the strategies below to help yourself implement a growth mindset in your everyday life.

- Visualize your dream
- Talk to your dream (seriously!)
- Promise yourself the best version of you
- Find a 30-day challenge to try something different and break up your routine
- Find inspiration in the success of others
- Refresh your routine
- Seek constructive feedback
- Use positive language
- Practice listening
- Learn something new
- Stay engaged

Highlight or circle one of the above strategies you'd like to try. Then, come back to this page and reflect on how it went.

_____
_____
_____
_____
_____
_____
_____

Try this...

It's important to take breaks throughout the day. Write YOU in to your schedule. Pencil YOU in each day for the next 4 weeks using the calendar below. Grow to give yourself more time. What will you do?

Example

Days of the Week

	M	T	W	Th	F	S	Su
Before 8 am	Plan day 15 minutes	Meditate 15 mins	Journal 15 mins	Walk 20 mins	Affirmations 15 minutes	Savor coffee & quiet 30 minutes	Journal 15 mins
Before noon	Call contact 15 minutes	Research project 30 minutes	Write & mail thank you's 20 mins	Watch class 30 minutes	Read industry article take notes 20 mins	Watch class 30 minutes	Meal prep one hour
Before 5 pm	3 minute breath exercise	Lunch with friend one hour	Dance 20 mins	Put my face in the sun & breathe 10 minutes	Email contact 20 minutes	Get outdoor air 20 mins	Skincare 20 mins
Before 9 pm	Journal 15 mins	Read one hour	Call friend who is funny 15 mins	Read 20 minutes	Watch the sunset 20 mins	Do absolutely nothing 15 mins	Plan week 15 mins

Try this...
Get your life back.

These do not have to be hard. If you cannot figure out a way to give yourself 10 minutes or so, 3 to 4 times a day, we need to talk!
That's 40 minutes!
And this is YOUR life.

Days of the Week

	M	T	W	Th	F	S	Su
Before 8 am							
Before noon							
Before 5 pm							
Before 9 pm							

The Art of Gratitude

Gratitude is an important practice because it allows us to remember what is *truly* important in life. The more you express gratitude the more you receive to be grateful for!

What is in your life that you can show gratitude for?

The Art of Gratitude

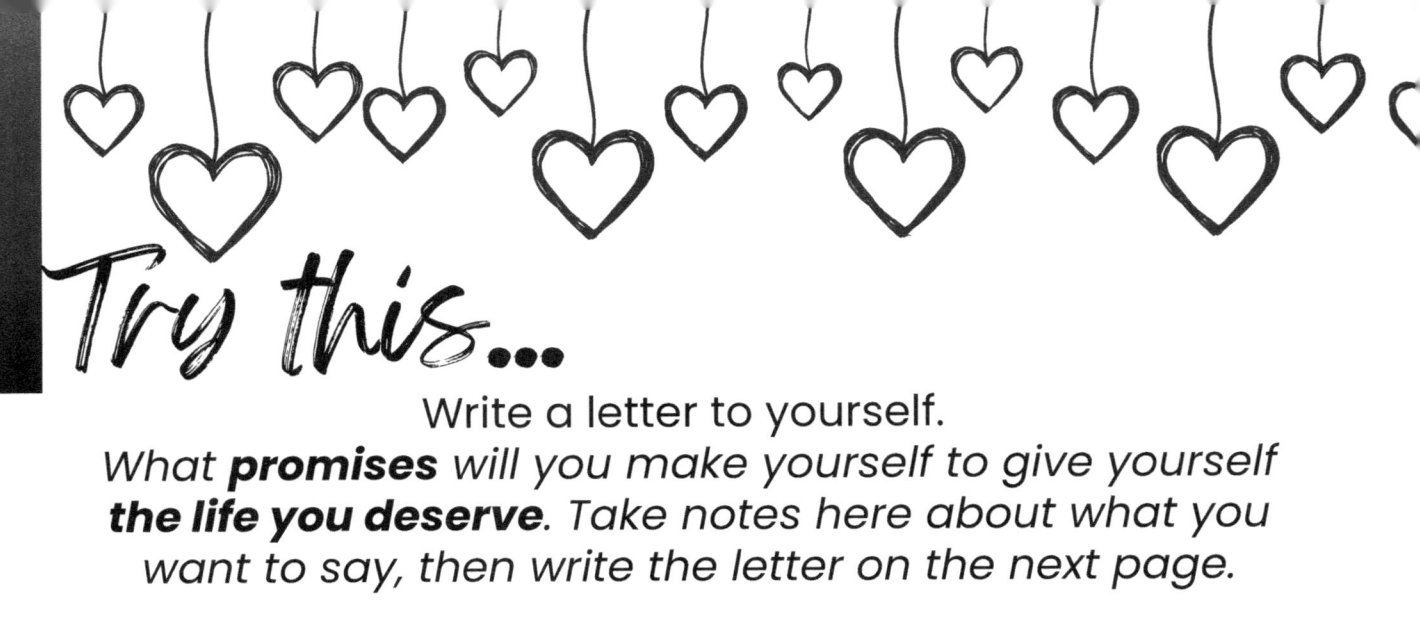

Try this...

Write a letter to yourself.
What **promises** will you make yourself to give yourself ***the life you deserve***. Take notes here about what you want to say, then write the letter on the next page.

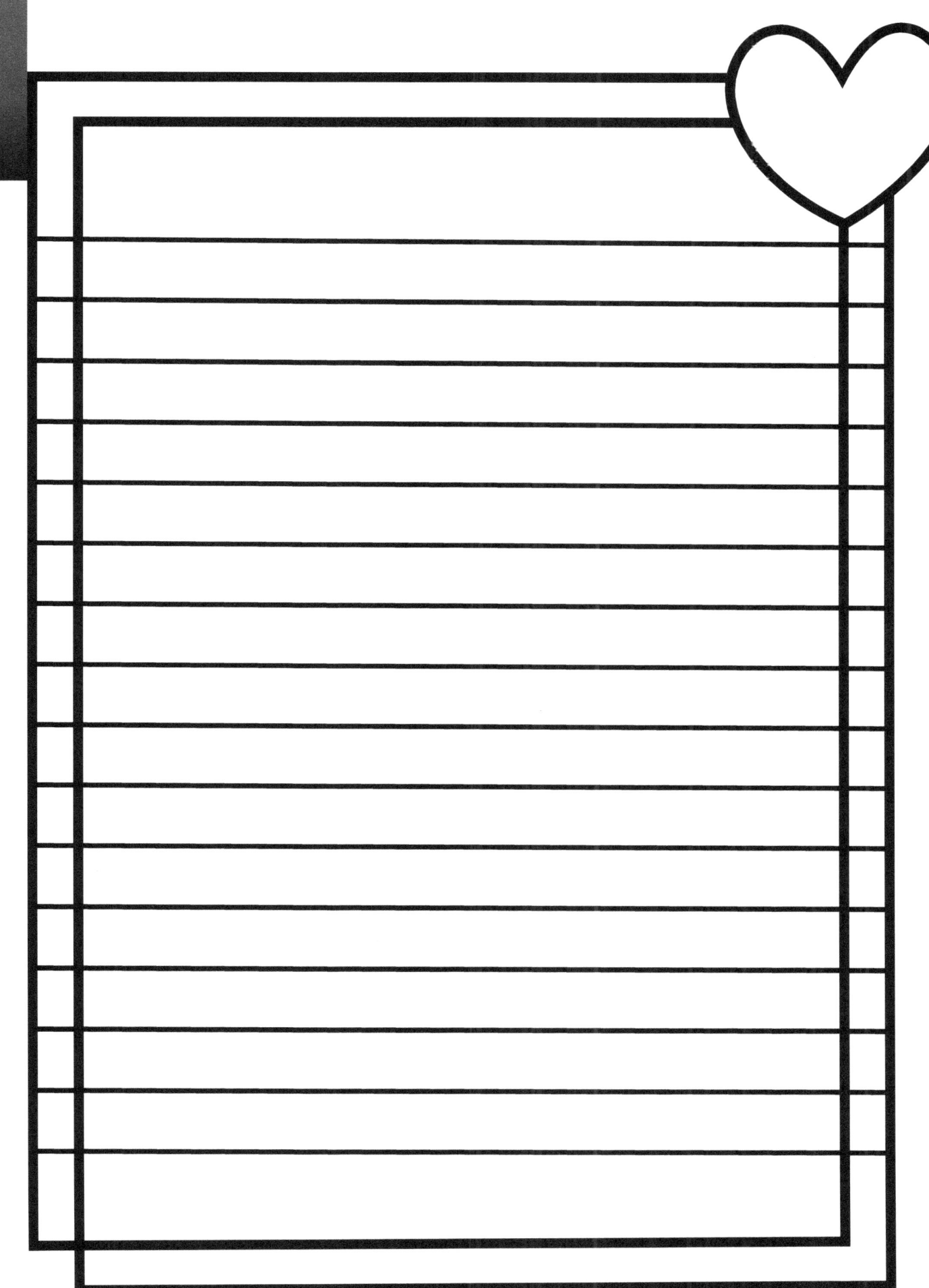

My Legacy

What used to inspire you?

_____
_____
_____
_____
_____

What did your dreams look like when you were a kid?

_____
_____
_____
_____
_____

My Legacy

What do you want your legacy to be?

_____
_____
_____
_____
_____
_____

What does your current life look like? What aligns with your vision and what does not?

_____
_____
_____
_____
_____
_____

My Purpose

You have purpose.
Your life and **your** hopes matter.

I believe I have purpose because...

_____
_____
_____
_____

I believe my life has meaning because...

_____
_____
_____
_____

I believe my dreams are valid because...

_____
_____
_____
_____

My Passion

How do you find your passion?

___
___
___
___

How do you grow your passion and turn it into something that **lifts** you?

___
___
___
___

What can your passion do **for you**?

___
___
___
___

Dream Brainstorming

Spend 10 minutes writing down all the dreams you can think of *without any judgment or filtering.*
Write them all down here.
Use the blank pages in the back of the book if you need more room. (I hope you do! ☺)

Take the Next Step

The statement, "just take the next step," is mentioned many many times in the book. Why do you think that one phrase is repeated so many times?

_____
_____
_____
_____
_____
_____

What is the power in you taking the next step and what will *your* next step be?

_____
_____
_____
_____
_____
_____

The Make a Way Mindset

The number one question I get, by far, is,
"How do you do it?"
For years I could not put the formula into words. I could only give the answer, "**I made a way**".

Turns out the formula was not really complicated at all.

Here's the big secret.

The formula is:

One Step + The Next Step x The Power of Positivity = Way Made

It also helps to believe in something bigger than yourself. I call Him God. You may call this higher power something else: Allah, Hashem, Jehovah, Universe or Source, to name some, not all by any means.
I don't get into names because all these faiths believe that there is something greater than us. Something that calls our hearts to *be* greater, serve others, and live our lives to the fullest.
Tap into something that is bigger than you.

Believe that your steps will be **rewarded**.
Take the first step, then the next.

Make a Map

Where are you going? Break your dream into doable tasks on a regular basis. Starting with your dream, to your goal, to the tasks needed to make your dream a reality.

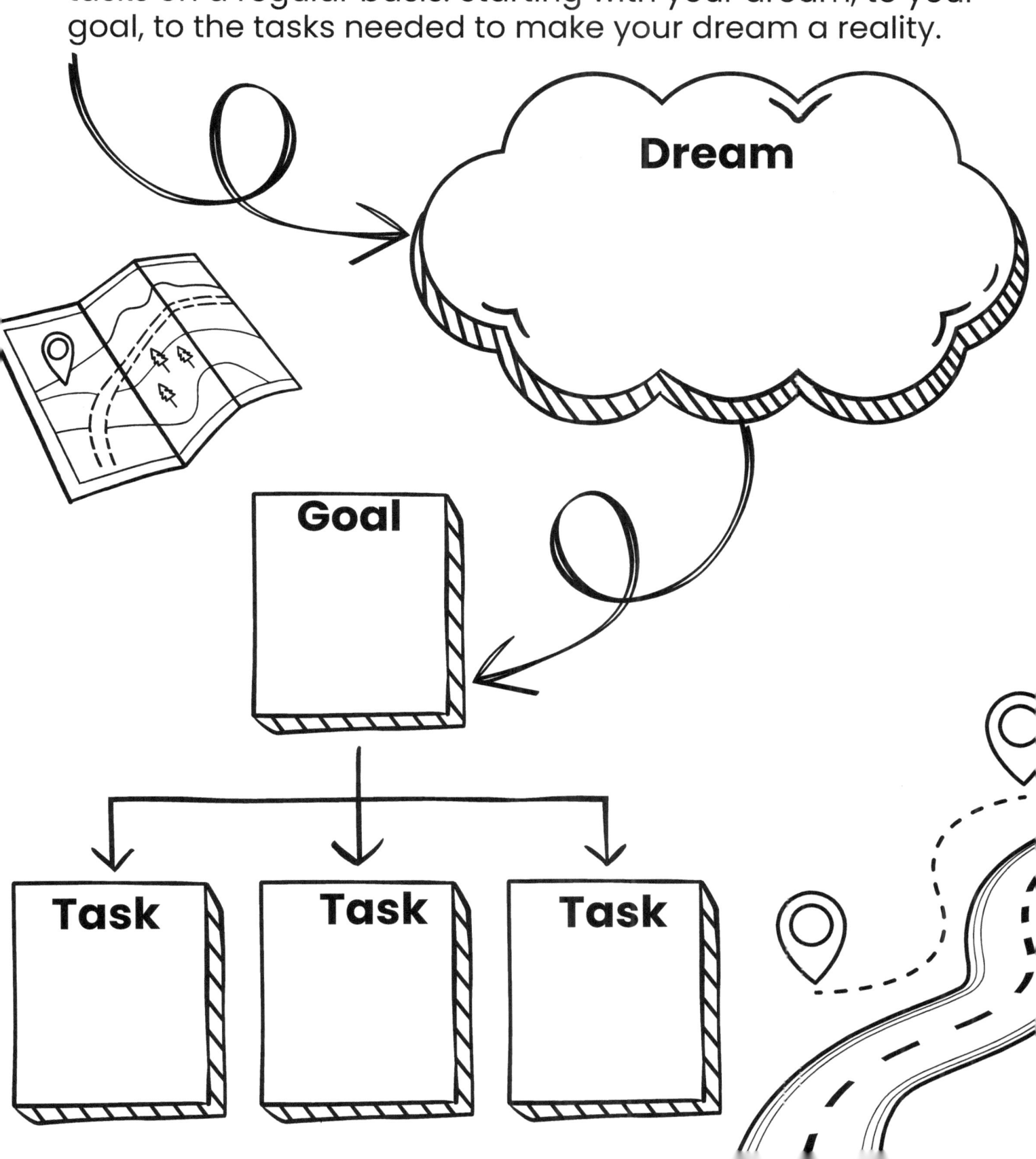

Make an Action Plan

How to make your goals SMART!

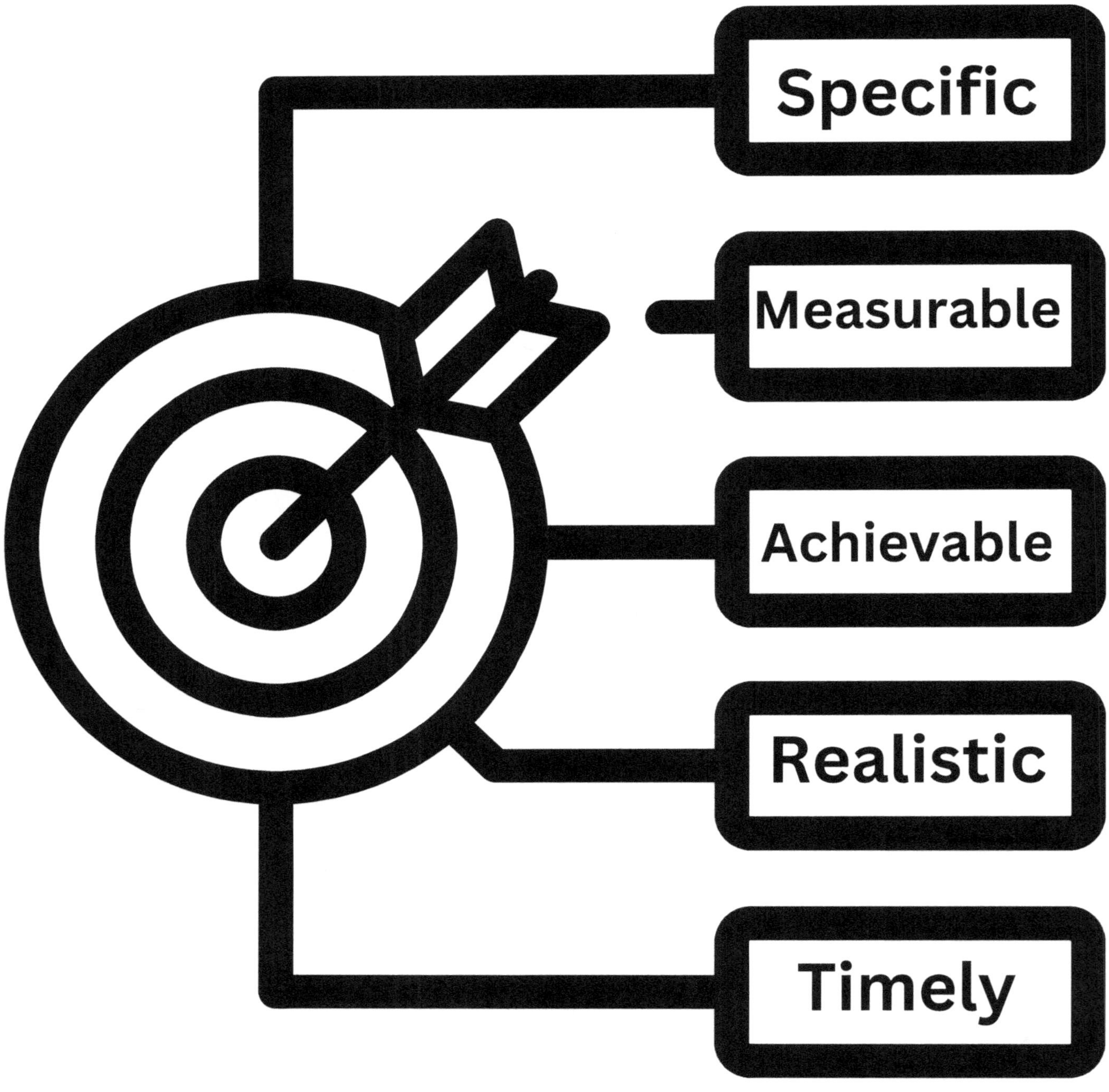

- **Specific**
- **Measurable**
- **Achievable**
- **Realistic**
- **Timely**

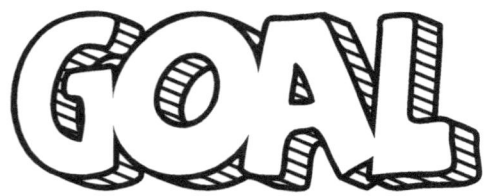  Notice I am starting off with the first draft- not a finished book!

Practice making your goal SMART!

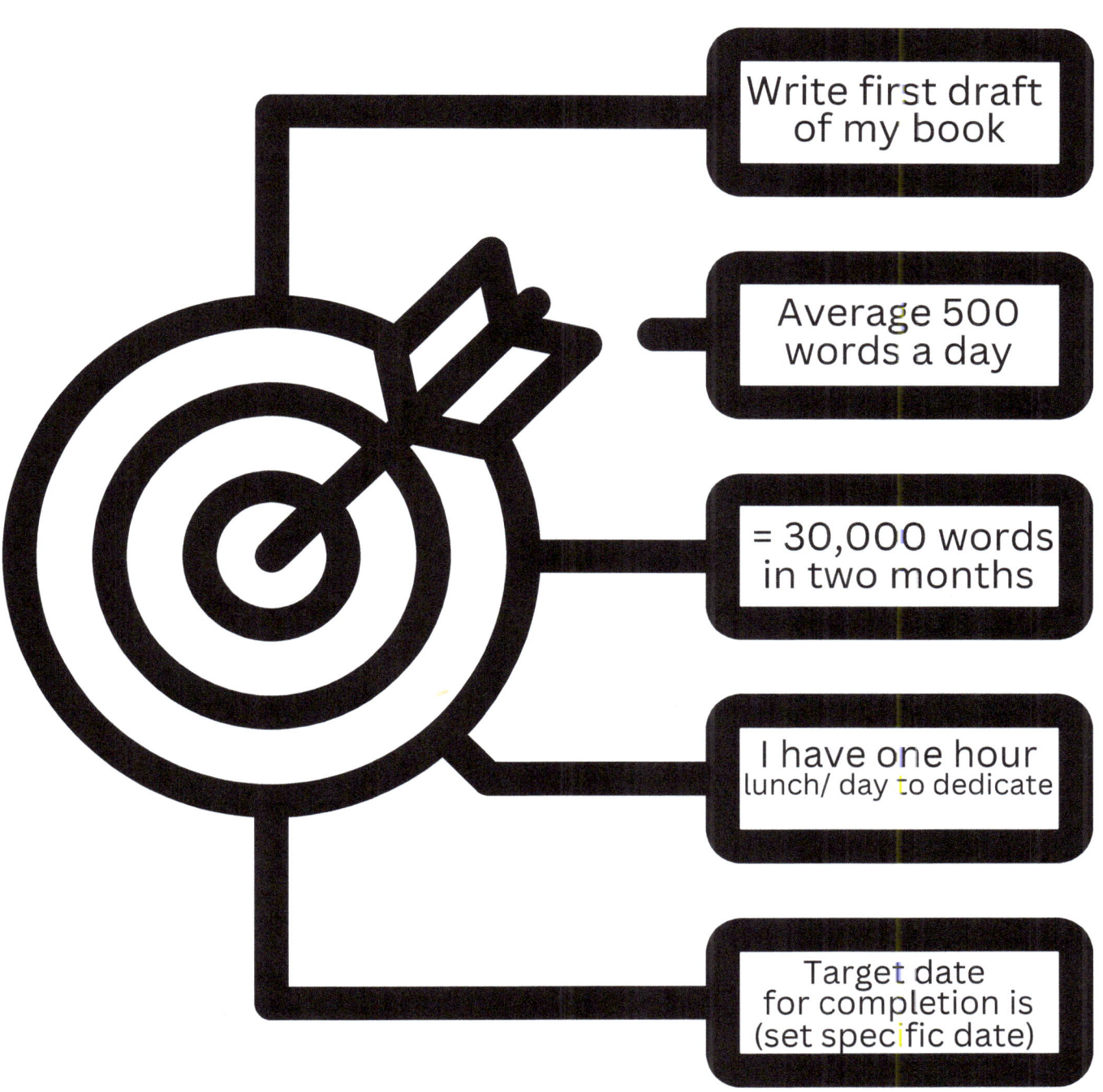

- Write first draft of my book
- Average 500 words a day
- = 30,000 words in two months
- I have one hour lunch/ day to dedicate
- Target date for completion is (set specific date)

Your goal must be something you can *realistically* do and you must set a target date to drive yourself to meet the deadline. Otherwise the goal is too open-ended and lacks accountability. Be specific with what you will do to meet the goal. **You got this!**

Practice making your goal SMART!

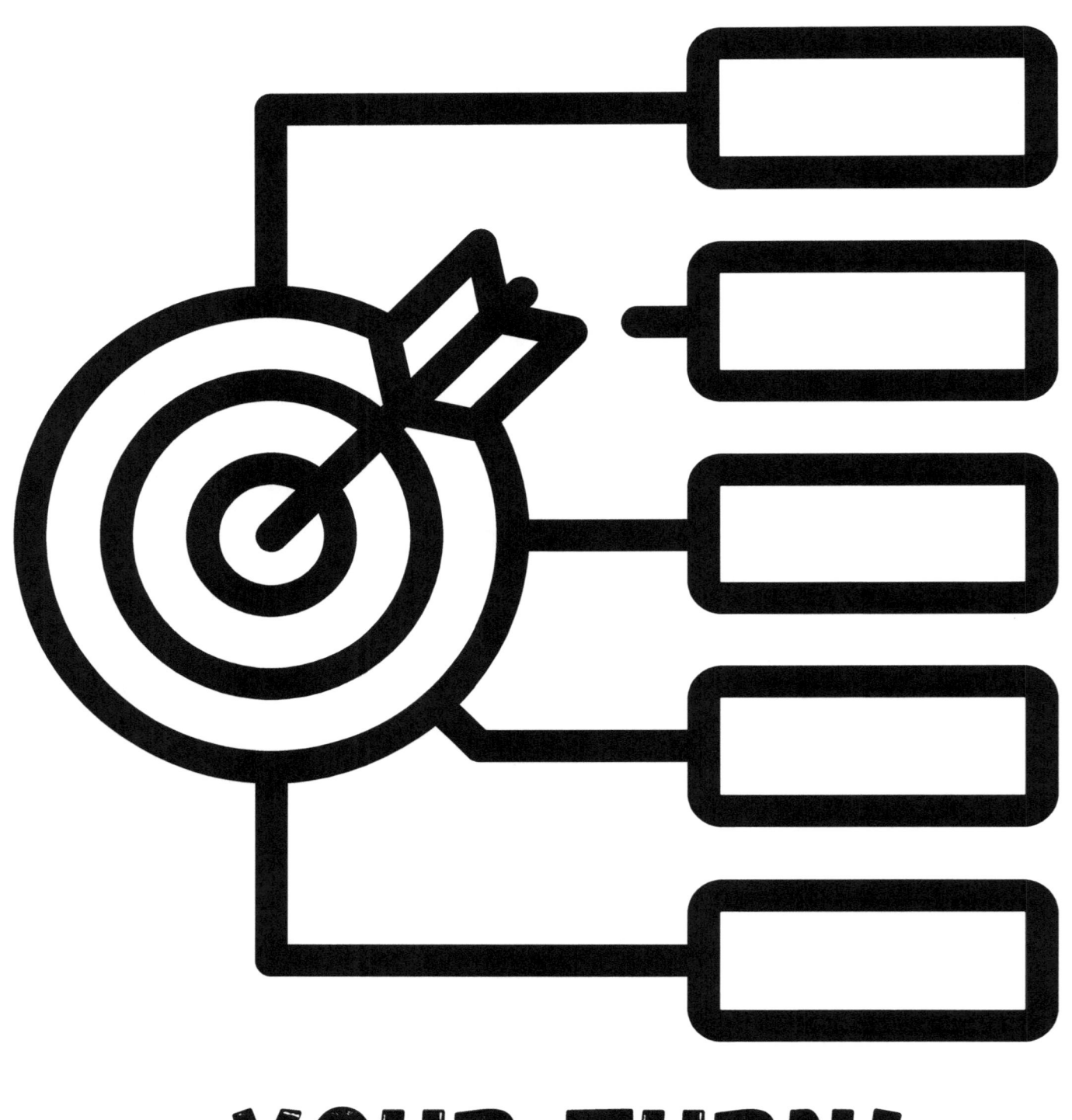

YOUR TURN!

Prioritize Tasks

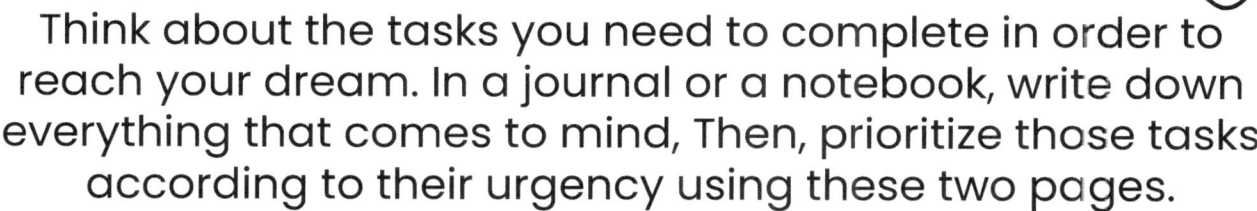

Think about the tasks you need to complete in order to reach your dream. In a journal or a notebook, write down everything that comes to mind, Then, prioritize those tasks according to their urgency using these two pages.

1. _____

2. _____

3. _____

4. _____

5. _____

6. _____

7. _____

8. _____

9. _____

Prioritize Tasks

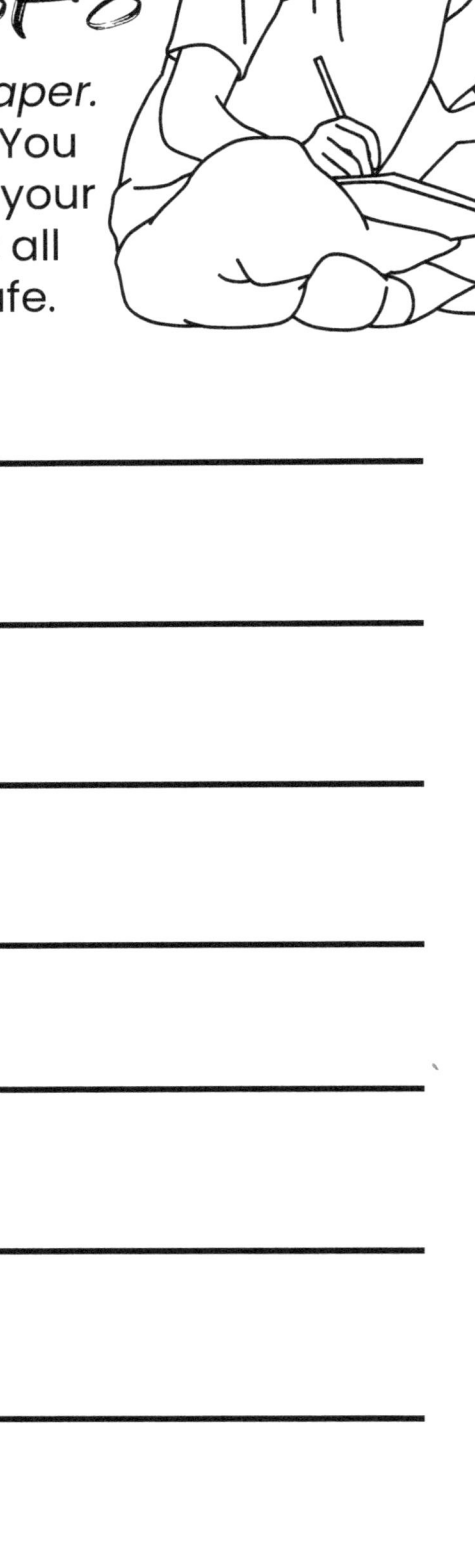

Get it out of your head and onto paper. That helps you take the stress off. You don't have to leave it all swirling in your head. And you don't have to do it all right now. Put it here where it's safe.

10 _____

11 _____

12 _____

13 _____

14 _____

15 _____

16 _____

17 _____

18 _____

Taking the next step

Part of your process for prioritizing might be to knock off things on the list you can do the easiest and the fastest.
This will help you build momentum.
Use the mind map to brainstorm your first three tasks you'll accomplish below.

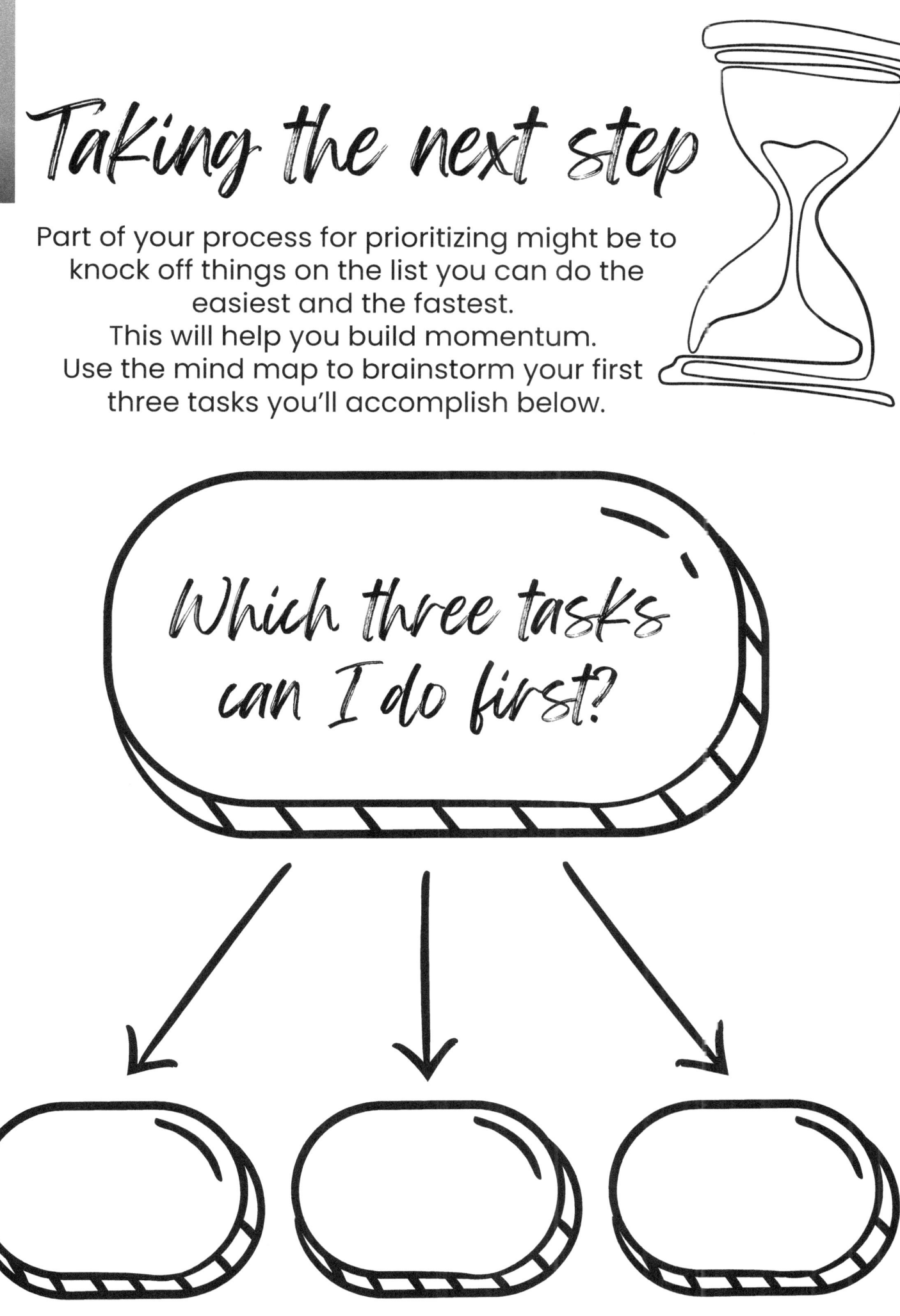

Finding Support

Making your dream a reality is hard work. It helps to have a good system of support as you work towards your dream. They'll remind you why you started the journey on hard days.

Identify different people below that you can turn to for support and how they help you.

On your team

Person	They help me by:

Motivation Journaling

What will it mean to you to achieve your dream?

Flag this page and review it often.

_____
_____
_____
_____
_____
_____
_____
_____
_____
_____
_____
_____
_____
_____
_____
_____

Motivation Journaling

What will it mean to you to achieve your dream?
Flag this page and review it often.

_____
_____
_____
_____
_____
_____
_____
_____
_____
_____
_____
_____
_____
_____
_____

List of Goals

Write goals for the next twelve months here. Then, come back to this page in 6 months and again in 12 months and check your progress.

Jan:

Feb:

Mar:

Apr:

May:

Jun:

Don't forget to celebrate!

List of Goals

Write goals for the next twelve months here. Then, come back to this page in 6 months and again in 12 months and check your progress.

Jul:

Aug:

Sep:

Oct:

Nov:

Dec:

Don't forget to celebrate!

Goal Reflection

What have I learned about myself over the last six months?

_____
_____
_____
_____
_____
_____

What have I learned about myself over the last twelve months?

_____
_____
_____
_____
_____
_____

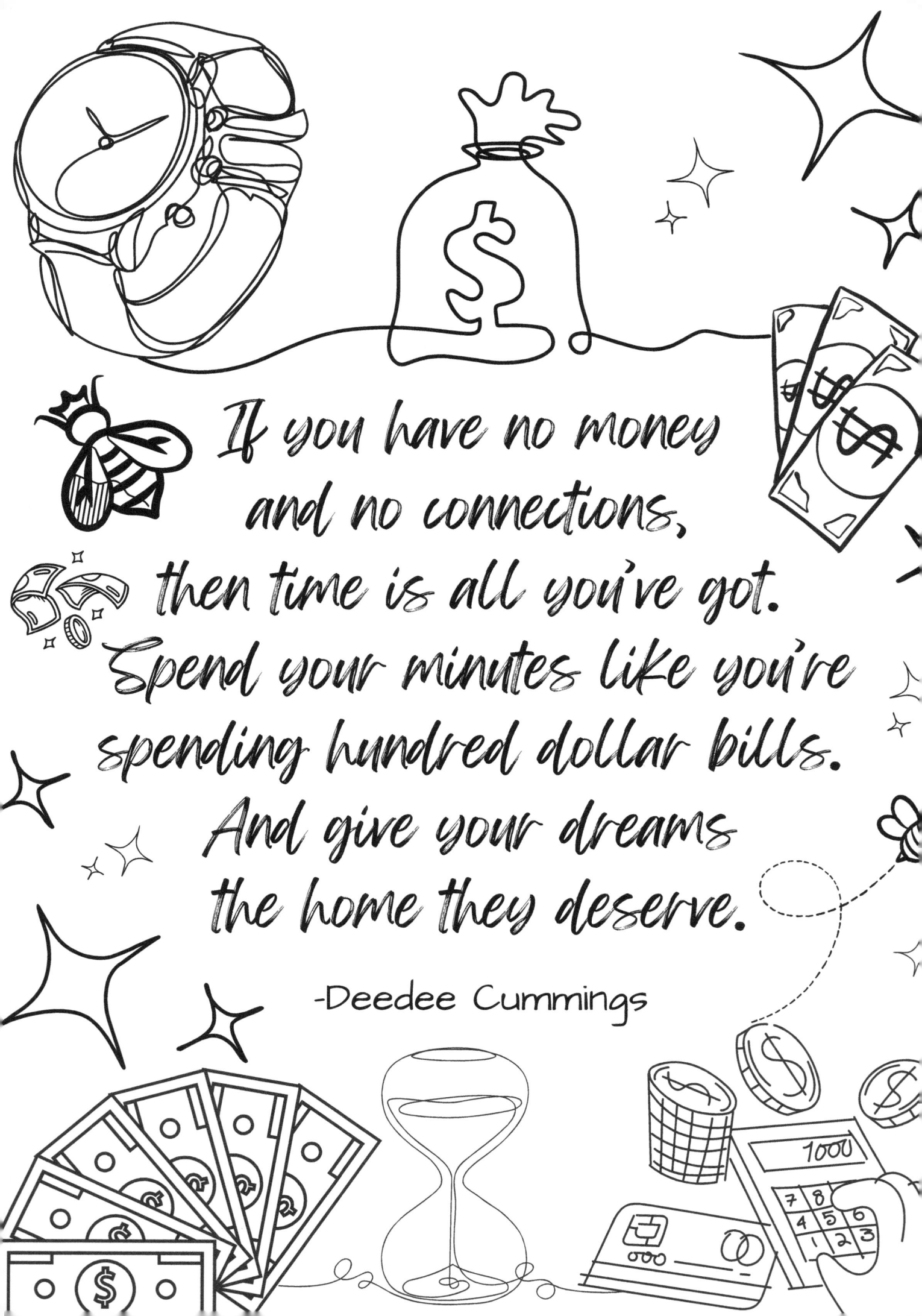

My Dreams are Within Reach

When we tell ourselves that our dreams are within reach, we begin to believe it!

Write personal affirmations that resonate with you and your dream below.

_____

_____

_____

_____

_____

Affirmation Sentence Stems...

- I deserve...
- I am worthy of...
- I am proud of...
- I love...
- I make...
- I am talented at...
- I am strong because...
- I am confident because...

The 10 Year Reach

We want everything overnight or next week. Life does not work like that. In the context of dreams, life is very long.
You have the time!
Even if you do not actually achieve the "big" dream ... say getting a show to Broadway, you still win! Effort will be rewarded. Motion in conjunction with a plan will be rewarded.

Time moves. There is nothing you can do to stop it, slow it down, or turn it back.

What could the next 10 years look like for you if you stayed in motion?

You at 30	You at 40
No house	Homeowner
No vacation to the beach	Vacation
Beaten down/tired/depressed	Lifted/engaged/excited
No retirement savings	Working on retirement savings
No generational wealth to pass down	A plan for wealth coming in or on the way
Feeling unfulfilled	Feeling rewarded for effort
No hope	Hope in spades

The 10 Year Reach

One thing we know for sure: ten years *will* pass!
Have you thought about your 10-year reach?
More importantly, have you written it down?
Because here's another thing about time, when you are
not documenting the journey, time gets away from you.
And it can get away from you *quickly*.

**Use the chart below to document your next
10 years of your life.**

Me at _____	Me at _____

Kickstart your Dream Engine!

CONGRATULATIONS!
If you have made it to this page you are well on your way and your dream is already in motion.

Hold on to these powerful truths:

- **Listen to your heart.**
- **You are not too late.**
- **You have all the time you need.**
- **Everything you want is within your reach.**
- **The only thing you need to be confident in is you.**
- ***You can do this.* Dreams happen every day.**
- **The goal is not to be rich or famous. The goal is to be *free*.**

Plant a Tree

Remember ... *you are planting a tree*. People will sit in the shade you provide for decades. Write the names or groups of people that your dream supports and inspires.

How to Dream Reflection

Reflect on and write about the biggest lessons you have learned from both the book **How To Dream** and the workbook.

_____
_____
_____
_____
_____
_____
_____
_____
_____
_____
_____
_____
_____
_____

"You are a human being with limitless potential. Everything you need is within your reach. Go get it."

-Deedee Cummings

Appendices

Gratitude log

Extra journaling sheets

BONUS coloring sheets- great for mindfulness, overthinking & stress relief

Annual goals review template

SMART Goals sheet

Timeline worksheet

Dream-Goal-Tasks worksheet

Lessons Learned log

Get your life back scheduling helper

Deedee's Dream Affirmations

Deedee's Dream Quotes

My dreams list extra pages for MORE dreams

The Art of Gratitude

Keep it going! Make it a part of your routine to document your blessings and all that you are grateful for. Gratitude is an important practice because it allows us to remember what is *truly* important in life.
What is in your life that you can show gratitude for?

_____
_____
_____
_____
_____
_____
_____
_____
_____
_____
_____
_____
_____
_____

The Art of Gratitude

The Art of Gratitude

Keep it going! Make it a part of your routine to document your blessings and all that you are grateful for. Gratitude is an important practice because it allows us to remember what is *truly* important in life.
What is in your life that you can show gratitude for?

_____
_____
_____
_____
_____
_____
_____
_____
_____
_____
_____
_____
_____
_____

The Art of Gratitude

Let's Journal!

**Keep documenting the journey.
Never stop learning.**

Let's Journal!

Let's Journal!

_____

_____

_____

_____

_____

_____

_____

_____

_____

_____

_____

_____

_____

_____

_____

_____

Let's Journal!

Let's Journal!

Let's Journal!

Let's Journal!

_____
_____
_____
_____
_____
_____
_____
_____
_____
_____
_____
_____
_____
_____
_____
_____

Let's Journal!

List of Goals

Write goals for the next twelve months here. Then, come back to this page in 6 months and again in 12 months and check your progress.

Jan:

Feb:

Mar:

Apr:

May:

Jun:

Don't forget to celebrate!

List of Goals

Write goals for the next twelve months here. Then, come back to this page in 6 months and again in 12 months and check your progress.

Jul:

Aug:

Sep:

Oct:

Nov:

Dec:

Don't forget to celebrate!

Practice making your goal SMART!

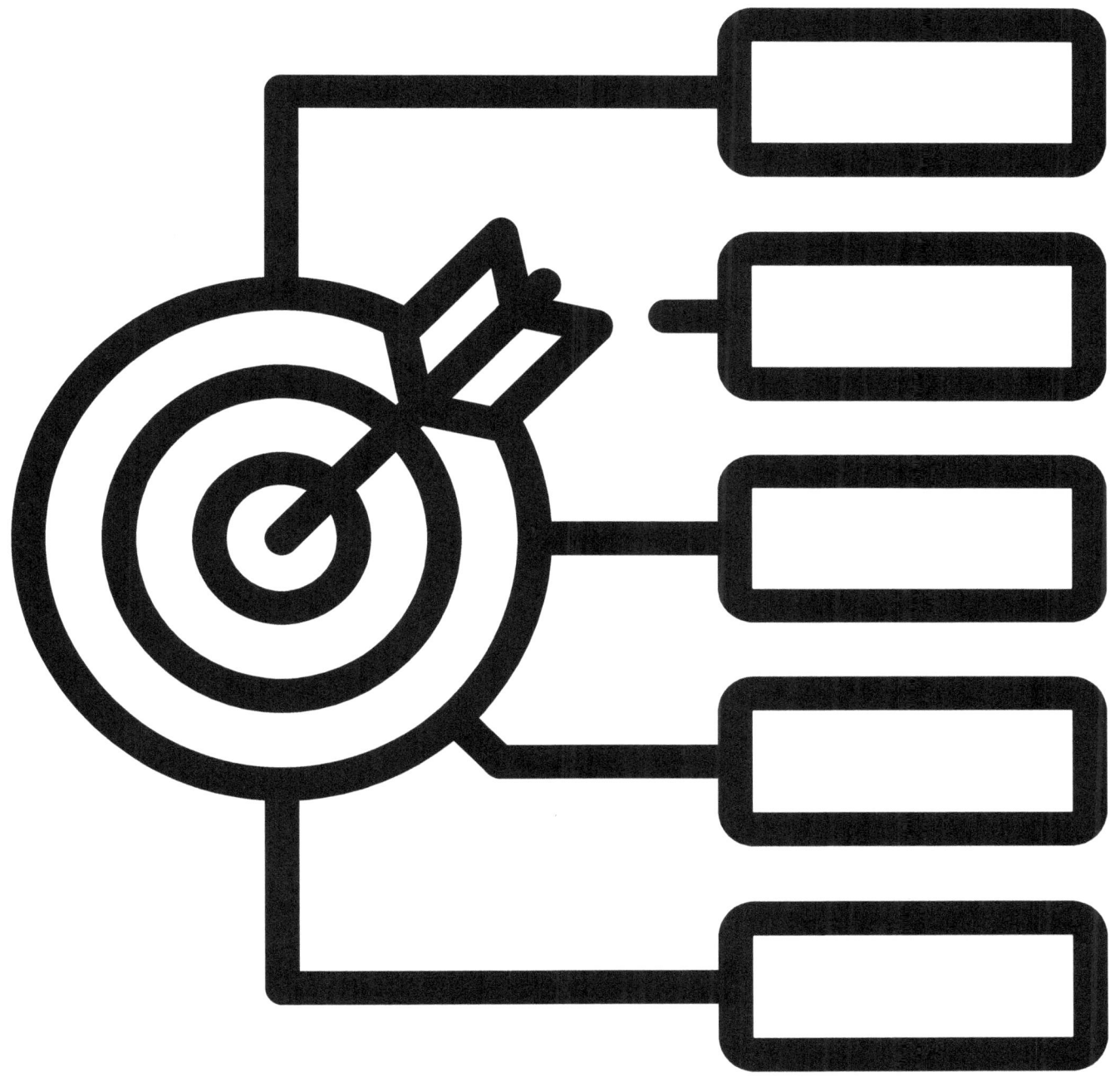

PLAN YOUR NEXT GOAL

Practice making your goal SMART!

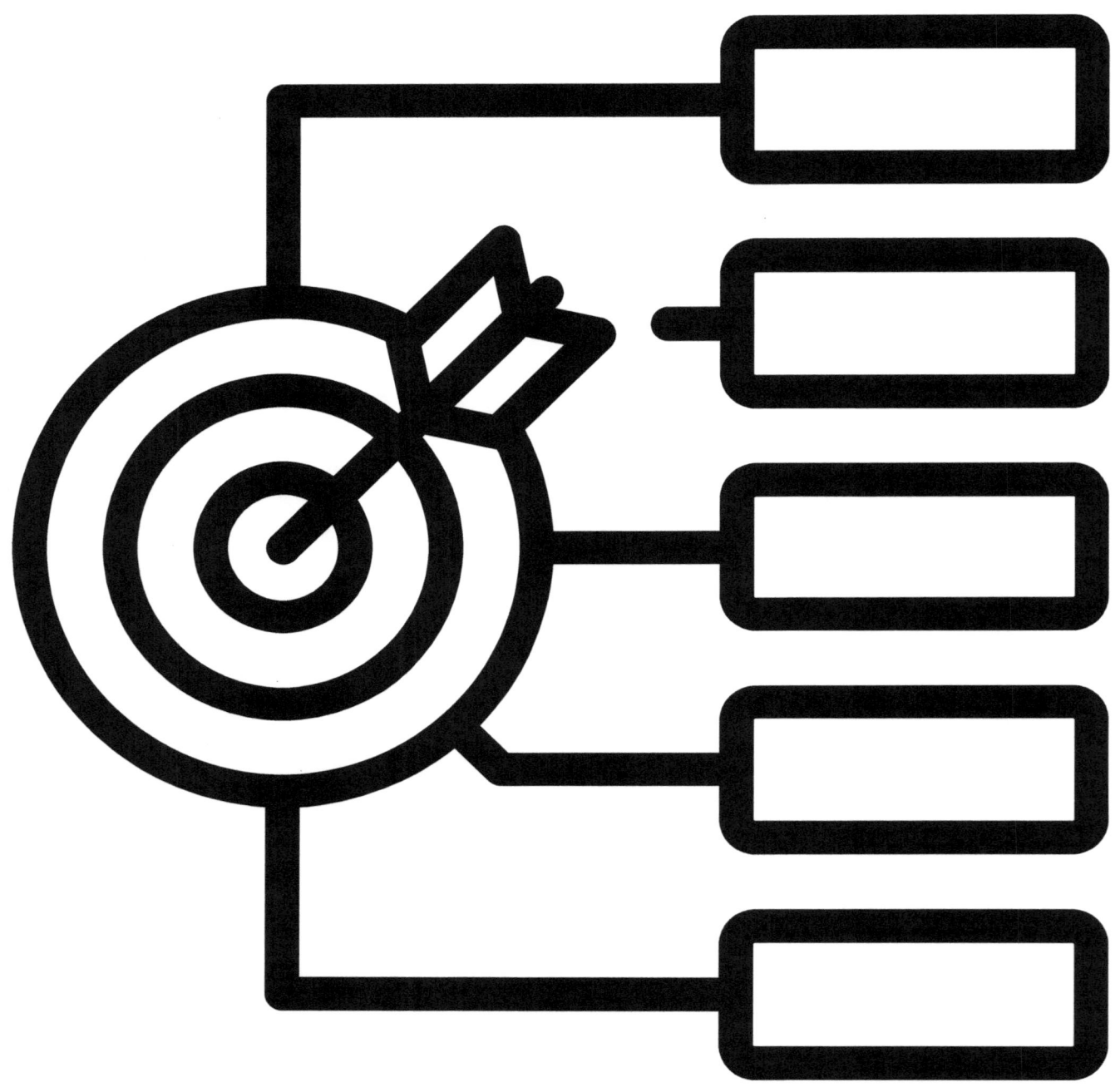

PLAN YOUR NEXT GOAL

Make a Timeline

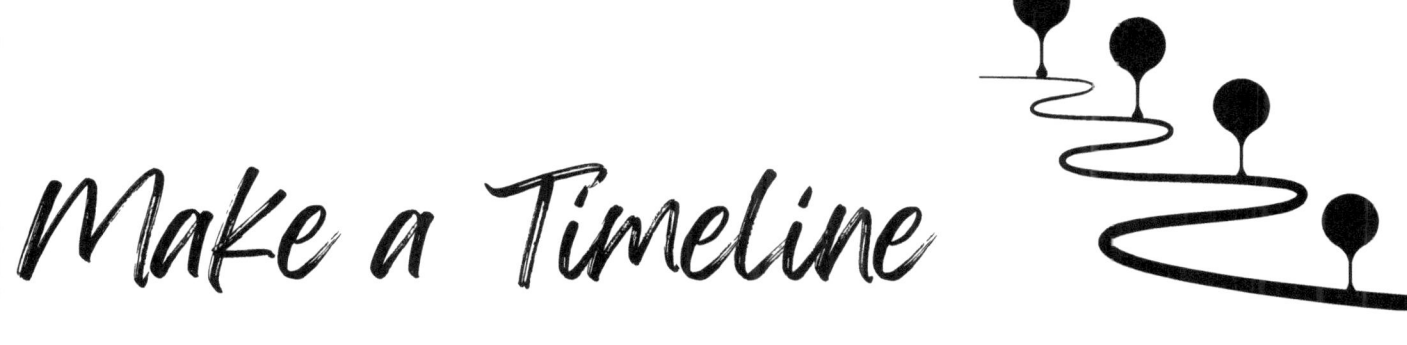

You need a timeline, so time does not get away from you, as time does. Let's plot your dream below. **Add a month or year with a goal in each box.** *This is accountability.*

Copyright © 2024. Deedee Cummings. *How to Dream: The Workbook*. All rights reserved.

Make a Map

Where are you going? Break your dream into doable tasks. Starting with your dream, to your goal, to the tasks needed to make your dream a reality.

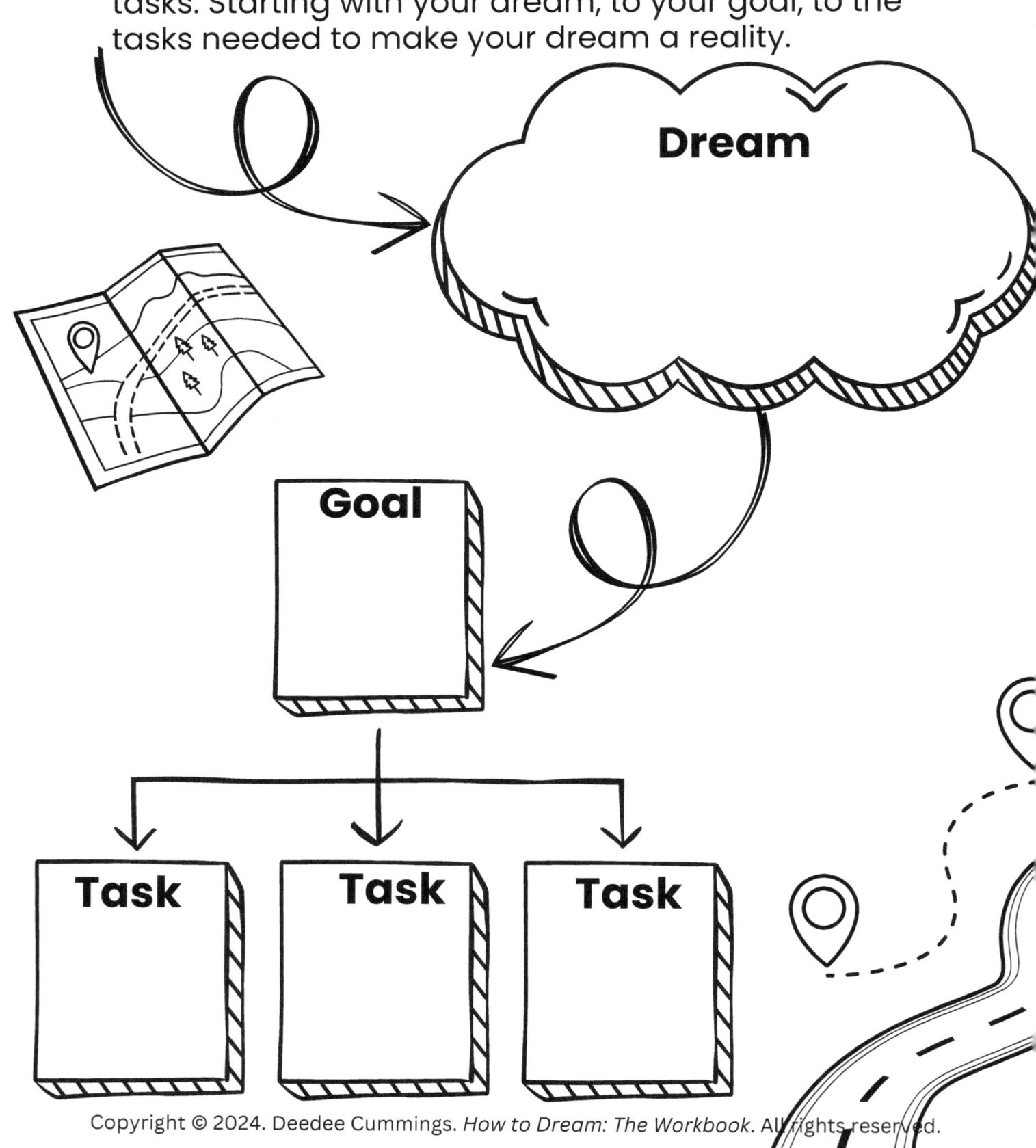

Lessons Learned

We have not talked about this elsewhere in the workbook, but this will be a helpful tool. Be sure not to ruminate on bitter experiences. That is not the point. However, document here some of the lessons you have learned along the way to help you stay focused.

I'll give you one of mine...
A lesson I learned a long the way is to keep going after my dream even when I'm the only one who shows up. After all, I am the only one who really needed to be there. I'm gonna KEEP showing up!

What lessons are you learning?

_____

_____

_____

_____

_____

_____

_____

_____

Lessons Learned

> Stay positive.
> Stay grateful.
> Lessons learned are obstacles removed.

_____

_____

_____

_____

_____

_____

_____

_____

_____

_____

Lessons Learned

> Stay positive.
> Stay grateful.
> Lessons learned are obstacles removed.

_____

_____

_____

_____

_____

_____

_____

_____

_____

Try this...

Get your life back.

	M	T	W	Th	F	S	Su
Before 8 am							
Before noon							
Before 5 pm							
Before 9 pm							

Days of the Week

Deedee's Dream Affirmations

I am dedicated to going after my dream.

I am worthy of success and freedom.

Every day I take a step closer to my goals.

I am resilient, determined, and unstoppable.

I believe in my vision.

I will not apologize for wanting more.

I will not apologize for having ambition.

I attract opportunities that align with my goals.

Everything I want is on its way to me.

I make room in my life for success.

I don't see problems, I see pathways.

I embrace challenges because they lead to growth and improvement.

I am planting a tree.

My hard work and dedication are paying off.

When I follow my heart, I am free.

Deedee's Dream Quotes

Your dream is your most cherished aspiration. Protect it, care for it, nurture it, talk to it, feed it, and love it like you would your favorite human being.

I can't think of anything scarier than not exploring your own life.

If you are reading these words, take this as your sign from the universe that you were destined to live a big life filled with big dreams.

Taking action on your dreams is a crucial part of your self-care.

Having fun with the dream is the only way to see the potential that might exist behind the vision.

Your dream will reveal beautiful, fun, and spontaneous parts of yourself you never even knew existed—parts of your mind, soul, and spirit that only a good dream can wake up.

If you feel unworthy of pursuing your dreams, then your very freedom has been taken from you. Your dreams have been hijacked!

Add therapists to the list of people you have in your circle to care for you.

Failure is a necessary part of success.

The *message* fear brings is never as bad as the *feeling* fear brings.

Copyright © 2024. Deedee Cummings. *How to Dream: The Workbook*. All rights reserved.

Deedee's Dream Quotes

There will never be time for you to follow your own ideas about what your life should be, unless you demand it and decide that **you alone** are a worthy priority.

Nothing clears noise like focus.

The world is loud. Your dreams have to be louder.

Your brain is a rich garden where all kinds of good stuff grows. Instead of tomatoes and cabbage, your brain grows ideas.

Don't ever take advice from people who have small dreams.

Nothing blocks noise like taking action.

You already have all the sticktoitiveness inside you that you will ever need.

Practicality is a dream killer.

Dreams make you unstoppable.

Your dream is a *cherished aspiration*. Love it like you would a dear sister. Nurture it like a child. Date it like a partner. Talk to it like you would a trusted friend.

Come out from behind four walls and look to the skies. There are answers there, waiting on you. Dreams can't reach you in a cubicle.

Dreams reveal your true potential.

Picture in your mind everything you want your life to be and then ensure every action you take moves you towards that vision.

Deedee's Dream Quotes

If you feel like you have no time for yourself, that is precisely the reason you must make the time. Life will continue to absorb everything you have. Intentionally plan to give *something* to yourself.

If you ask someone for help and they say no, be grateful that they did. *They were not meant to be a part of your story.*

She took care of her dream, and her dream took care of her.

Failure is not an end. Failure is a portal.

You need that failure. It will make you better. If nothing else, it will damn sure remind you of where you never want to be again.

Sometimes the journey is more the goal than the goal itself. Take the journey.

Make a way. And a way *will* be made for you.

Don't tell me *no*. Tell me *how*.

Are you gonna move full speed ahead? Then you're gonna need to toughen up. Your muscles need weights. Your brain needs words.

Dreaming is freedom of the mind, heart, and soul.

Believe you *can* and you will be absolutely right. Believe you *can't* and you will also be just as right. Which right do you want to be?

When I follow my heart, I am free.

If the dream finds you, so will the way.

Deedee's Dream Quotes

If you have no money and no connections, then time is all you have. Spend your minutes like you are spending hundred dollar bills.

Time moves. There is nothing you can do to stop it, slow it down, or turn it back. The only thing you can do is move right along with it.

You will never feel completely ready to do the thing you are about to do. Do it anyway.

Not giving up is the only way you can truly test whether or not your dream is real.

I am planting a tree.

Be careful what you feed your mind. It will become your *default* and it will come back to visit you over and over again.

Growth is motion. Working on your mind is an important part of putting your dream in motion.

The only barrier is your mind and the fear and negativity you let live there.

When you find your purpose, days when no one shows up hurts less. You are confident. You are passionate. You are living in your purpose. The only person who needed to show up that day was you.

Copyright © 2024. Deedee Cummings. *How to Dream: The Workbook.* All rights reserved.

Deedee's Dream Quotes

Life is not a merry-go-round. You are not strapped in on the only horse that was left to grab. You are an active participant in your life. You are in control of this ride. Act like it!

Don't measure your journey by the journey of anyone else. It's not about becoming the best version of Jay-Z. It's about becoming the best version of you. Jay-Z is the best version of Jay-Z.

It's not about making a billion dollars either. *It's about being free.* Anything else that comes with it is gravy.

*You are a human being filled with **limitless** potential.* You have **can do** power that has been divinely gifted to you. But **can do** power is nothing with a **can't do** mindset. You need a growth mindset. **You need a Make A Way Mindset**.

A fixed mindset says: I am not good enough.
A growth mindset says: I am good enough, so that settles that.

Dreamers are bold. Dreamers are in motion. Dreamers are a little cocky.

You are UNSTOPPABLE.

Never stop dreaming.

Copyright © 2024. Deedee Cummings. *How to Dream: The Workbook.* All rights reserved.

Dream List

Write every dream you can think of here. Do so without filtering, wondering, questioning, or judgment. Come back often. Keep going!

_____

_____

_____

_____

_____

_____

_____

_____

_____

_____

Dream List

Write every dream you can think of here. Do so without filtering, wondering, questioning, or judgment. Come back often. Keep going!

_____

_____

_____

_____

_____

_____

_____

_____

_____

_____

Dream List

Write every dream you can think of here. Do so without filtering, wondering, questioning, or judgment. Come back often. Keep going!

_____

_____

_____

_____

_____

_____

_____

_____

_____

_____

Dream List

Write every dream you can think of here. Do so without filtering, wondering, questioning, or judgment. Come back often. Keep going!

Two quick things you can do to help the world spread the word about the power of dreams:

1) Please leave a review wherever you bought this book or on Goodreads. It means the world to an author and only takes a minute!

2) Take your favorite quote and turn it into a social media post. Don't forget to tag me or **Make A Way Mindset** on Instagram!

Thank you for supporting this dream. I want to hear from you! Write to me at **deedee@makeawaymedia.com** and share your dream journey with me.

Never stop dreaming!
~Deedee

www.ingramcontent.com/pod-product-compliance
Lightning Source LLC
Chambersburg PA
CBHW041809070526
44586CB00025B/2814